Vamos a contar / Counting Books

3,2,1 ¡VAMOS!

Contemos hacia atrás
usando el transporte

3,2,1 GO!

A Transportation Countdown

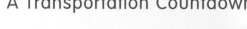

por/by Sarah L. Schuette

Consultora de lectura/Reading Consultant:
Jennifer Norford
Consultora Senior/Senior Consultant:
Mid-continent for Research and Education

CAPSTONE PRESS
a capstone imprint

A+ Books are published by Capstone Press
1710 Roe Crest Drive, North Mankato, Minnesota 56003.
www.capstonepub.com

Library of Congress Cataloging-in-Publication Data
Schuette, Sarah L., 1976–
 [3, 2, 1, go! Spanish & English]
 3, 2, 1 ávamos! : Contemos hacia atrás usando el transporte = 3, 2, 1, go! : a transportation countdown/
por/by Sarah L. Schuette.
   p. cm.—(Vamos a contar = Counting books)
 Includes index.
 Summary: "Counts backward from ten to one starting with ten school buses and ending with one city
bus—in both English and Spanish"—Provided by publisher.
 ISBN 978-1-4296-8249-7 (library binding)
 1. Counting—Juvenile literature. I. Title. II. Title: 3, 2, 1, go! III. Title: Three, two, one, go!
QA113.S388718 2012
513.211—dc23   2011028674

Credits
Strictly Spanish, translation services; Jason Knudson, designer; Eric Manske, bilingual
   book designer; Gary Sundermeyer, photographer; Laura Manthe, production specialist

Note to Parents, Teachers, and Librarians
3, 2, 1, ¡Vamos!/3,2,1 Go! uses color photographs and a nonfiction format to introduce children to various
modes of transportation while building mastery of basic counting skills in English and Spanish. It is
designed to be read aloud to a pre-reader or to be read independently by an early reader. The images
help early readers and listeners understand the text and concepts discussed. The book encourages further
learning by including the following sections: Glossary, Internet Sites, and Index. Early readers may need
assistance using these features.

Printed in the United States of America in North Mankato, Minnesota.
102011   006405CGS12

How many toys sit on the shelf?

¿Cuántos juguetes hay en la repisa?

10

TEN toy school buses

School buses take children to and from school.

DIEZ autobuses de juguete

Los autobuses escolares llevan a los niños de ida y vuelta a la escuela.

4

NINE toy ambulances

Ambulances hurry to accidents.

NUEVE ambulancias de juguete

Las ambulancias se apuran a llegar a accidentes.

EIGHT toy train cars

Train cars travel on railroad tracks.

OCHO vagones de tren de juguete

El tren y los vagones viajan en vías del ferrocarril.

7

SEVEN toy police cars

Police officers travel in police cars to keep towns and cities safe.

SIETE autos patrulleros de juguete

Los oficiales de policía viajan en autos patrulleros para mantener los pueblos y las ciudades seguros.

SIX toy airplanes

Airplanes can soar in the sky.

SEIS aviones de juguete

Los aviones pueden volar en el cielo.

5

FIVE toy taxicabs

People ride around town in taxicabs.

CINCO taxis de juguete

La gente viaja en taxi alrededor de la ciudad.

4

FOUR toy tugboats

Tugboats pull barges in the water.

CUATRO remolcadores de juguete

Los remolcadores tiran de barcazas en el agua.

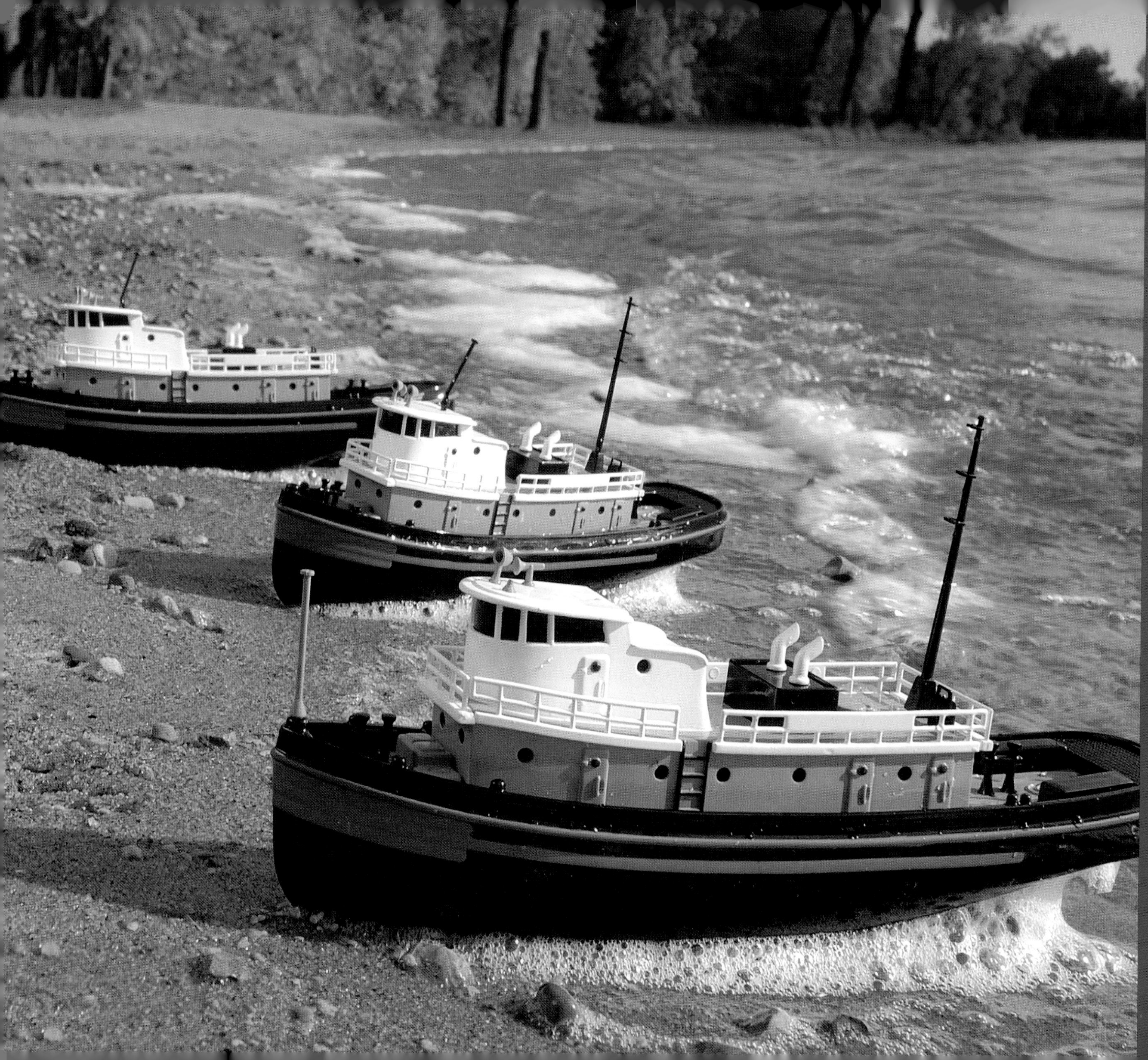

10
9
8
7
6
5
4
3
2
1
0

THREE toy dairy trucks

Dairy trucks deliver milk.

TRES camiones lácteos de juguete

Los camiones lácteos entregan leche.

2

TWO toy fire trucks

Firefighters ride in fire trucks.

DOS camiones de bomberos de juguete

Los bomberos viajan en camiones de bomberos.

1

ONE toy city bus

A city bus carries passengers around a city.

UN autobús de juguete

Un autobús lleva pasajeros alrededor de la ciudad.

How many toys have wheels?

How many toys have wings?

How many toys can float?

¿Cuántos juguetes tienen ruedas?

¿Cuántos juguetes tienen alas?

¿Cuántos juguetes pueden flotar?

Things That Go

Cosas que se mueven

school bus /
autobús escolar

ambulance /
ambulancia

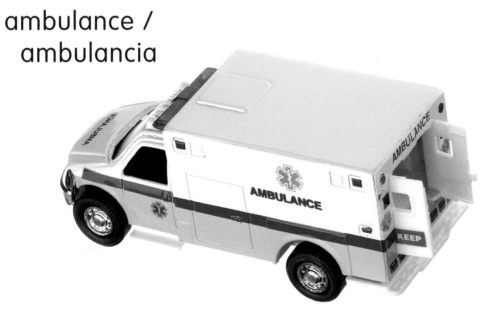

tugboat /
remolcador

26

dairy truck /
camión lácteo

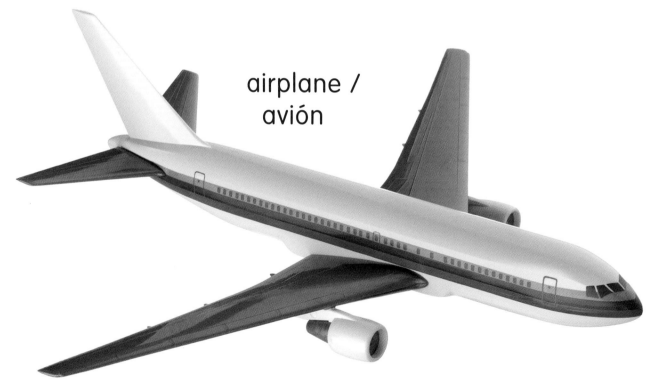

airplane /
avión

police car /
auto patrullero

train /
tren

fire truck /
camión de bomberos

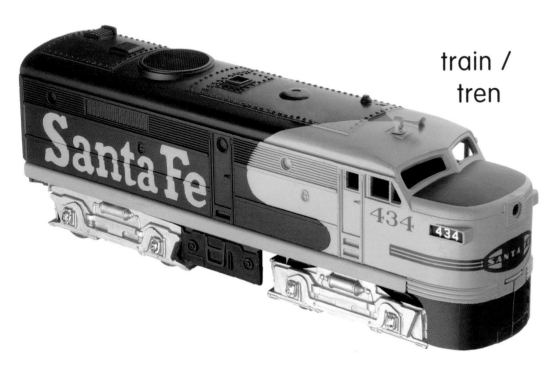

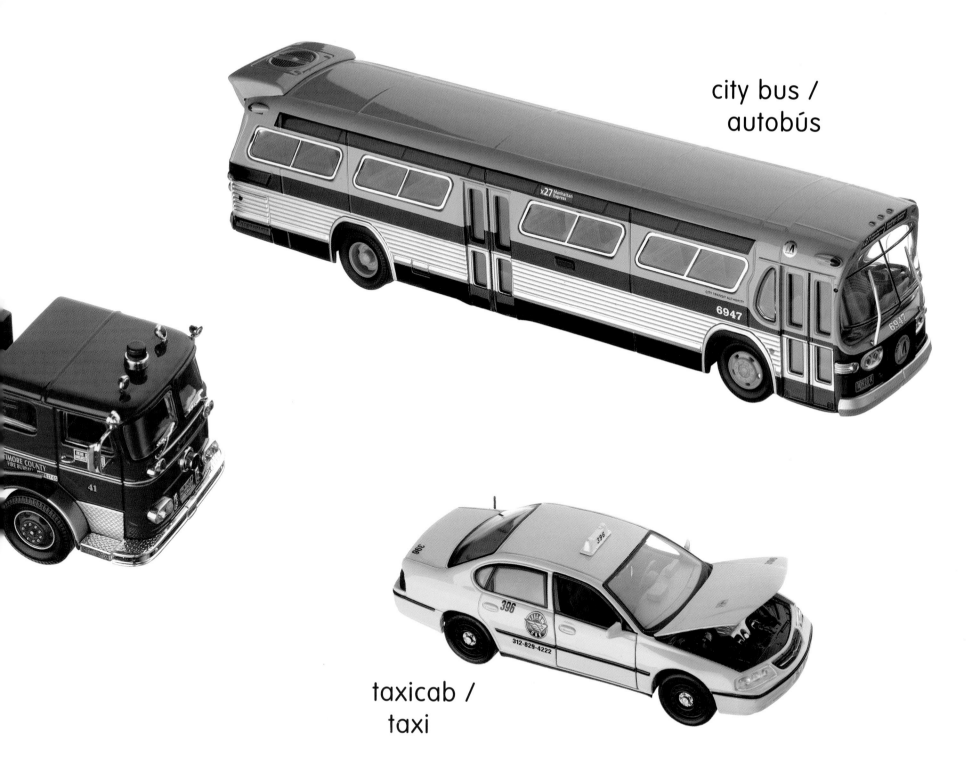

city bus /
autobús

taxicab /
taxi

29

Glossary

accident—something that takes place unexpectedly and that often involves people being hurt

barge—a long boat with a flat bottom; barges carry heavy cargo from place to place; barges are pulled by tugboats because they cannot move by themselves

dairy—a product made with milk; milk, cheese, and yogurt are dairy products

officer—someone who is in charge of other people; police officers are in charge of people's safety

passenger—someone besides the driver who travels in a vehicle; passengers ride in taxicabs, buses, and airplanes

soar—to fly high in the air

Internet Sites

FactHound offers a safe, fun way to find Internet sites related to this book. All of the sites on FactHound have been researched by our staff.

Here's all you do:

Visit *www.facthound.com*

Type in this code: 9781429682497

Glosario

el accidente—algo que ocurre inesperadamente y que a menudo involucra gente que se lesiona

la barcaza—un bote largo con un piso plano; las barcazas llevan cargas pesadas de un lado a otro; los remolcadores tiran de las barcazas porque no pueden moverse por sí solas

el lácteo—un producto hecho con leche; leche, queso y yogur son productos lácteos

el oficial—alguien que está a cargo de otras personas; los oficiales de policía están a cargo de la seguridad de la gente

los pasajeros—alguien además del conductor que viaja en un vehículo; los pasajeros viajan en taxis, autobuses y aviones

volar—elevarse alto en el cielo

Sitios de Internet

FactHound brinda una forma segura y divertida de encontrar sitios de Internet relacionados con este libro. Todos los sitios en FactHound han sido investigados por nuestro personal.

Esto es todo lo que tienes que hacer:

Visita *www.facthound.com*

Ingresa este código: 9781429682497

Index

Check out projects, games and lots more at
www.capstonekids.com

Índice

Hay proyectos, juegos y mucho más en
www.capstonekids.com